FOSTERING:
A benefits handbook

GW00683387

Adam Smith

BAAF
ADOPTION
& FOSTERING
www.baaf.org.uk

British Association for Adoption & Fostering
(BAAF)
Saffron House
6–10 Kirby Street
London EC1N 8TS
www.baaf.org.uk

Charity registration 275689 (England and Wales) and SC039337 (Scotland)

© Adam Smith, 2009

British Library Cataloguing in Publication Data
A catalogue record for this book is available from the British Library

ISBN 978 1 905664 25 2

Project management by Shaila Shah, Director of Publications, BAAF
Designed and typeset by Andrew Haig & Associates
Printed in Great Britain by T J International
Trade distribution by Turnaround Publisher Services, Unit 3, Olympia Trading Estate,
Coburg Road, London N22 6TZ

All rights reserved. Apart from any fair dealing for the purposes of research or private
study, or criticism or review, as permitted under the Copyright, Designs and Patents Act
1988, this publication may not be reproduced, stored in a retrieval system, or transmitted
in any form or by any means, without the prior written permission of the publishers.
The moral right of the author has been asserted in accordance with the Copyright,
Designs and Patents Act 1988.

BAAF is the leading UK-wide membership organisation for all those concerned with
adoption, fostering and child care issues.

Contents

The author

Adam Smith has worked as a benefits adviser for Kent County Council for more years than he cares to remember. His wife is a fostering social worker so this book, along with two children (Laurie and Matthew), is the obvious culmination of their efforts.

Acknowledgements

The author would particularly like to thank Eileen Fursland, his editor, for structuring his thoughts into a coherent whole, and Shaila Shah for the encouragement along the way. Thanks also to Colin Bent, Pat Collier, Doug Lawson and Samantha Sexton for their valuable input.

This book is dedicated to the foster carers of Kent – thank you for your inspiration.

Introduction

Deciding to become a foster carer will undoubtedly affect many aspects of your life – including your finances.

This book explores the relationship between social security benefits and tax credits and different types of fostering for foster carers.

It will help you to understand whether or not fostering a child will affect your eligibility for benefits and the amount you can claim. It also considers other types of financial help that you may be able to claim.

The book is divided into parts based on the different types of fostering. In each case, it looks at:

- the effect of fostering on all means-tested benefits, other earnings-replacement benefits and Child Benefit

- whether extra benefit can be paid for the child

- whether the fostering allowance will affect payment of the benefit

- whether fostering counts as work (there are some types of benefits that are affected by work and in some cases fostering may be seen as paid work)

- other miscellaneous effects.

It is intended as a short, easy-to-read guide, so it provides only the basic regulations of each relevant benefit. Not all benefits are mentioned (e.g. Retirement Pension) as there are some on which fostering has no effect.

This book is aimed primarily at foster carers in England and Wales, but much of the information is relevant to foster carers throughout the UK. It will also be helpful to social workers, fostering social workers, parents and anybody with an interest in placing children in other people's homes.

Please note that the figures, thresholds and other regulations quoted are correct at the time of going to press (spring 2009), but are liable to change in the future.

You can visit the government website, www.direct.gov.uk, for up-to-date information.

How to use this book

You don't need to read this book all the way through. Only two or three chapters are likely to apply to you.

You must read Chapter 1 because:

- it will help you understand which type of fostering you do and which parts of the book apply to you

- it outlines various benefits and tax credits and the rules that apply to them. You can refer back to this information as you read later chapters.

The rest of the book is separated into chapters which apply to different situations.

Use Chapter 1 and the chart below to find out which other parts of the book you need to read.

AT A GLANCE
Everyone must read Chapter 1.

If you have a child or children living with you and:

- they are "looked after" children – see Chapters 2 and 6

- they are your own children – see Chapter 9

- they are privately fostered – see Chapter 7

- there is a special guardianship order in force – see Chapter 5

- there is a residence order in force – see Chapter 5

- the child is not "looked after" but you are still paid – see Chapter 3

- you are fostering a parent and baby, one or both of whom are "looked after" – see Chapter 6

If the child also:

- has a disability – see Chapter 10

- is aged 16 or over – see Chapter 8

If you do not have a child or children living with you but:

- you provide respite care – see Chapter 4

- you provide day care – see Chapter 4

Fostering and your finances

1

Types of fostering

As a foster carer, you need to understand the legal status of the child you are caring for, because payment of benefits is often determined by the child's status.

Looked after children

A "looked after" child is a child who is in the care of the local authority. Under Section 23 (s23) of the Children Act 1989 (England and Wales), the local authority has a duty to provide accommodation (such as a foster home) for children it is looking after.

Children can become "looked after" in one of two ways:

- the child may be subject to a **care order**, which means a court has ordered that the child can be taken away from the parents because of abuse or neglect;

- the child may be **accommodated**, i.e. "looked after" on a voluntary basis by the local authority (for instance, because the parents have agreed they need some help or because the parents are ill, in hospital or have died).

Kinship or "family and friends" care

The term kinship or "family and friends" care is used to refer to circumstances in which children are in the care of a relative or family friend because the parents are unable or unwilling to look after the child themselves.

However, there are two types of kinship care and it's important to understand which applies in your case, as it can affect your benefit entitlement.

- **Formal kinship care**, in which the child is "looked after" under s23 of the Children Act 1989 (as above) and the local authority has arranged for relatives or friends of the family, who have been approved, to foster the child.

- **Informal kinship care**, which is an informal arrangement made with the support of the local authority but outside the looked after children system. The child is not "looked after" but the local authority provides financial and other support to the relatives and friends who are caring for the child.

Parent and baby placements

This is where a child and one or both of the child's parents are placed with a foster carer as a "package" by the local authority under s23. Either the child or the parent (or both) may be a looked after child. They stay with the foster carer full-time but generally for a fixed period, and the local authority pays the foster carer a fostering allowance.

Private fostering

Private fostering is a private arrangement by the child's parent or parents rather than by the local authority. The child is not "looked after". The definition of private fostering is that a child under 16 (or under 18 and disabled) is living with someone who is not a parent, a relative or a person with parental responsibility, or the local authority, and the period of care is intended to last for 28 days or more.

Day care

A small number of children need planned day foster care. They don't need to sleep at the foster home but do need the care and attention of a foster carer during the day, perhaps because they find attending school difficult or their parent needs extra help during the day.

Respite or short break foster care

Sometimes foster carers provide respite or short break care to support parents who may be struggling. For instance, parents of children with a disability often need a break from the demands of looking after their child or children so that they can catch up with other things, spend more time with other members of the family or have a rest or a holiday. Foster carers may provide respite care for a child in their own home for one weekend every month, for example.

Types of payment for foster carers

Financial support from local authorities

Local authorities give financial support to foster carers who look after children who are in the care system. (For foster carers who foster with independent fostering providers, this money will come to them via the agency.) Foster carers are paid an allowance which is seen as covering the cost of caring for the child; on top of this, many foster carers are also paid a fee which is seen as payment for their time and skills. Respite carers and informal kinship carers may also be given financial support.

For the purposes of working out benefits, it is not just the type of fostering you do that matters but also the type of financial support you are given.

As a general rule, local authorities make payments to foster carers according to various sections of the Children Act 1989:

Looked after children

Section 31 applies to children subject to a care order and **Section 20** applies to children who are accommodated.

Your entitlement to welfare benefits and other financial help is exactly the same in both of these cases.

This situation is covered in Chapter 2. When it is a parent and baby placement and one or both are looked after children, see Chapter 6.

Fostering children who are not "looked after"

Section 17 payment is often given in situations where children are not "looked after" but the local authority is involved in setting up and supporting the arrangement outside the looked after children setting. For instance, it may be given to support informal care arrangements in which members of the child's extended family or friends foster the child. It is also often given to foster carers providing respite care and day care. These situations are covered in Chapters 3 and 4.

Residence orders and special guardianship

There are two other types of allowance that may be paid by the local authority in certain cases:

Residence order allowances are paid when informal kinship or "family and friends" carers have taken out a residence order (a court order stating where and with whom a child shall live).

Special guardianship allowances are paid when carers – foster carers or family and friends carers – have been granted a special guardianship order. This is a court order intended to provide legal permanence for children who cannot live with their birth families. In some cases, the special guardian continues to receive some payment for fostering, in addition to the maintenance element of the fostering payment, for some time after the order is made. These situations are covered in Chapter 5.

Private fostering payments

In private fostering arrangements, it is the child's parents, rather than the local authority, who pay the carers with whom their child will live. This is covered in Chapter 7.

Benefits and allowances

The benefits and tax credits system can be separated into:

- Means-tested

- Contributory

- Non-means-tested and non-contributory

MEANS-TESTED BENEFITS

Although these benefits all have different rules, the one thing they have in common is that they are determined by your means or resources: the more income you have, the less benefit you get. However, some income is not taken into account, which is why you need to understand the implications of your fostering.

Many of these means-tested benefits will be affected if your savings go above £16,000 (savings above £6,000 can reduce the amount of benefit you can claim). Savings include bank and building society accounts and so you should be aware that any unspent income accumulating in your account can affect your benefits.

Income Support

What is it?
Income Support is the benefit payable to you and your family if you have a low income and are unable to work because of caring responsibilities. It is based on your income and/or capital.

Who is it for?
You must meet the following criteria:

- you have savings of no more than £16,000;

- you are not in full-time work (this means you, as the claimant, can work up to 16 hours a week and your partner may work up to 24 hours);

- you are not in full-time education;

- you are aged 16–59;

- you have caring responsibilities, i.e. you are a single parent, a foster carer or caring for someone with a severe disability;

- you are on a low income.

NB: Changes have recently been made to the benefit system which will affect single parents who make new claims. From 24 November 2008, their entitlement to Income Support stops when their youngest child reaches age 12. From 26 October 2009, it will stop when their youngest child reaches age 10; and from 25 October 2010, when their youngest child reaches seven. However, single people who have a **foster child** living with them, who is under the age of 16, are **exempt** from these changes and can claim Income Support.

How to claim
Claims for Income Support are mainly done over the telephone on 08000 556688.

Housing Benefit

What is it?

This is the benefit to help people on a low income with their rent. Again, it is based on your income and/or savings.

Who is it for?

You must meet the following criteria:

- you have savings of no more than £16,000 (unless in receipt of the guarantee credit element of Pension Credit – see page 14);

- you have rent to pay;

- you are on a low income.

How to claim

Claims should be made from the local council, i.e. your local authority.

Council Tax Benefit

What is it?

This is the benefit to help people on a low income with their council tax payments. Again, it is based on your income and/or capital.

Who is it for?

You must meet the following criteria:

- you have savings of no more than £16,000 (unless in receipt of the guarantee credit element of Pension Credit – see page 14);

- you are liable to pay council tax;

- you are on a low income.

How to claim
Claims should be made from the local council.

Jobseeker's Allowance

What is it?
This is the benefit for people of working age who are unemployed and are available for work and cannot claim Income Support.

Who is it for?
You must meet the following criteria:

- you have savings of no more than £16,000 (for income-based Jobseeker's Allowance); or

- you have the correct national insurance record (for contribution-based Jobseeker's Allowance);

- you are not in full-time work (i.e. you may work for up to 16 hours a week and your partner, if you have one, may work for up to 24 hours);

- you are not in full-time education;

- you are aged between 16 and 60 (women) or 65 (men);

- you are available for and actively seeking work and have a "jobseeker's agreement" (which you have agreed with your local Job Centre).

How to claim
Claims for Jobseeker's Allowance are mainly done over the telephone on 08000 556688.

Employment and Support Allowance

What is it?

Employment and Support Allowance (which replaced Incapacity Benefit in October 2008) provides an income for people who cannot work due to illness or disability.

The entitlement conditions are:

- contribution-based;
- income-related.

CONTRIBUTION-BASED

Who is it for?

You must meet the following criteria

- you have paid sufficient national insurance contributions;
- you are incapable of work due to sickness or disability.

INCOME-RELATED

Who is it for?

You must meet the following criteria:

- you have savings of no more than £16,000;
- you are not in full-time work (16 hours for claimant or 24 hours for the partner);
- you are not in full-time education;
- you are aged 16–59;
- you are incapable of work due to sickness or disability;
- you are on a low income.

How to claim

Claims for Employment and Support Allowance are mainly done over the telephone on 08000 556688.

Pension Credit

What is it?

This is for people aged 60 and over. It is intended to "top-up" the state retirement pension. However, like many of the benefits discussed in this booklet, it is means-tested – based on your income and/or capital.

Who is it for?

You must meet the following criteria:

- you are aged 60 or over (guarantee credit) or are aged 65 or over (savings credit);

- you are on a low income.

How to claim

Claims should be made to the Pensions Service helpline on 0800 991234.

CONTRIBUTORY BENEFITS

Contributory benefits are based on a person's national insurance record. For the purposes of this book there are only two that are relevant.

Employment and Support Allowance

What is it?

This benefit provides an income for people who cannot work due to illness or disability.

Who is it for?

You must meet the following criteria:

- you must be incapable (or treated as incapable) of work;

- you must have the correct national insurance record (or qualify as somebody incapable of work in youth).

How to claim
Claims for Employment and Support Allowance are mainly done over the telephone on 08000 556688.

Incapacity Benefit

This benefit has now been abolished for new claims (and replaced by Employment and Support Allowance (ESA) – see above), but people who were already claiming it before October 2008 can continue to do so. Claimants will be moved over to ESA in the next few years.

NON-MEANS-TESTED AND NON-CONTRIBUTORY BENEFITS
These benefits are based on neither your resources nor your national insurance record. Other factors determine whether you qualify.

Child Benefit

What is it?
This is what is called a "universal" benefit. Child Benefit is paid irrespective of your income and/or capital. It is not payable for a child if you receive a fostering allowance for the child's care.

Who is it for?
You must meet the following criteria:

- you must have a child (aged under 16 or, in certain circumstances, under 20) living with you; or

- you contribute towards the maintenance of the child; and

- you have priority over other potential claimants.

How to claim

Claims should be made by contacting the Child Benefit helpline on 0845 302 1444.

Guardian's Allowance

What is it?

An extra benefit paid to people who are looking after other people's children (notice that this is not the same as special guardianship described on p. 53).

Who is it for?

You must meet the following criteria:

- be entitled to Child Benefit for the child you are looking after; and

- both parents of the child have died or one has died and you do not know where the other parent is, or one has died and the other is detained in prison or in hospital.

How to claim

Telephone the Guardian's Allowance Unit on 0845 302 1464.

Carer's Allowance

What is it?

This benefit is paid to carers who look after severely disabled people.

Who is it for?

You must meet the following criteria:

- you must be aged 16 or over (there is no upper age limit but it is not payable if you receive certain other benefits, e.g. Retirement Pension);

- you must provide care for at least 35 hours a week;

- the person for whom you provide care gets Disability Living Allowance care component at the middle or higher rate or Attendance Allowance.

How to claim

Telephone the Carer's Allowance Unit on 01253 856123 and request a form.

Disability Living Allowance

What is it?

A benefit to help with the extra costs of being disabled and which has two components: care component and mobility component.

Who is it for?

The child or adult with the disability must meet the following criteria for the care component:

- they need help or encouraging with aspects of personal care: dressing, washing, taking medication, communicating, eating, toileting, etc, or they need supervising to ensure they are not a danger to themselves or other people; and

- these care needs have existed for at least three months; and

- these care needs are likely to last for another six months; and

- in the case of a child, these care needs are far in excess of the normal requirements of a child of the same age; and

- if you are claiming for a child, he or she must be at least three months old.

The child or adult with the disability must meet the following criteria for the mobility component:

- be unable or virtually unable to walk, or be deaf and blind, or a double amputee, or severely mentally impaired; or, if aged three years old and above, have severe behavioural problems; or

- require guidance or supervision when walking in unfamiliar places and (in the case of a child aged five and above) the mobility needs are far in excess of the normal requirements of a child of the same age; and

- these mobility needs have existed for at least three months; and

- these mobility needs are likely to last for another six months.

How to claim
Contact the Benefit Enquiry Line on 0800 882200 to request a form.

Child Trust Fund

For all children born on or after 1 September 2002, the Government will pay £250 into a Child Trust Fund account (and again when the child turns 7) for people who receive Child Benefit. There are special arrangements for looked after children.

Contact the Child Trust Fund Helpline on 0845 302 1470.

Education Maintenance Allowance

After the age of 16 some young people can claim an Education Maintenance Allowance worth up to £30 a week, designed to encourage them to stay on at school or college. All looked after children are entitled to the full amount. For your own children, it is dependent on your income. Only taxable income is taken into account so a fostering allowance and section 17 payments do not affect it.

To apply, the young person should ask their school or college for an application form or telephone the Government's Learner Support Helpline on 0800 121 8989.

Other help

Disabled facilities grant

What is it?
To help meet the cost of adapting a property for the needs of a disabled person.

Who is it for?
The owner occupier or tenant applies but the grant is to help the disabled person live in the property. It is not means-tested if the application is made by the guardian (including foster carers) of a child with a disability.

How to claim
Contact your local council.

Exemption from road tax

What is it?
All vehicles have to pay road tax, but some disabled people can apply for exemption.

Who is it for?
The child or adult must be getting the high rate of the mobility component of Disability Living Allowance

How to claim
Contact the Pension, Disability & Carers Service on 08457 123456 and request the relevant form.

Motability scheme

What is it?
The provision of a fully insured car.

Who is it for?
The person (or child, if you are claiming on behalf of a child) must be getting the high rate of the mobility component of Disability Living Allowance with at least one year left to run on the award.

How to claim
Contact Motability on 0845 456 4566.

Tax relief and tax credits

Extra tax relief for foster carers

Foster carers can claim extra tax relief. The limit is currently £10,000 per residence a year plus £250 a week for each child aged 11 and over and £200 a week for each child aged under 11. If your fostering payments are less than this individual limit, you will be exempt from tax. If your income from fostering payments is above the individual limit, you will be taxed on all income above the limit.

Contact the Self-Assessment Helpline on 0845 900 0444.

Child Tax Credit

What is it?
This is a benefit introduced in April 2003, administered by Her Majesty's Revenue & Customs, for people (whether working or not) who have children. It is dependent on your income.

Who is it for?
You must meet the following criteria:

- you must have a child (aged under 16 or, in certain circumstances, under 20) living with you;

- your income is less than £66,000 pa.

How to claim
Telephone the Tax Credit helpline on 0845 300 3900.

Working Tax Credit

What is it?
This is a benefit introduced in April 2003, administered by Her Majesty's Revenue & Customs, for people on a low income who are working. It is dependent on your income. If you have children, it is paid in addition to Child Tax Credit.

Who is it for?
You must meet the following criteria:

- you work at least 16 hours a week;

- you are on a low income;

- you fit into one of the following four criteria:

    1. you are responsible for a child; or

2. you have a disability that puts you at a disadvantage in getting a job; or

3. you are aged 25 years or over and working at least 30 hours a week, or

4. you are aged 50 or over and recently unemployed or sick.

How to claim
Telephone the Tax Credit helpline on 0845 300 3900.

National insurance for foster carers

As a foster carer you may choose to be classed as self-employed if you wish. If you are self-employed you have to pay Class 2 national insurance contributions on your earnings unless you are exempt from liability due to low earnings. However, you will get credits (instead of having to pay) in the following circumstances:

- signing on as unemployed;

- sending in medical certificates;

- being in receipt of, or with an underlying entitlement to, Carer's Allowance.

Approved foster carers get "home responsibility protection" for the tax years 2003/4 onwards. This reduces the number of years of contributions needed to get Retirement Pension and bereavement benefits.

Home Responsibilites Protection is to be abolished as per the Pension Act 2007. This is effective from 6 April 2010 and for foster carers there will be the chance to make weekly contributions through the new system. For more information, visit www.thepensionservice.gov.uk/pensions-reform/act.asp, and look under Parents and Carers.

How to claim

Booklet SE1 (including form CWF1) is available from Orderline on 0845 900 0404 or can be downloaded from www.hmrc.gov.uk.

For more information on National Insurance and being self-employed, visit www.hmrc.gov.uk/migrantworkers/self-employed.htm.

Help with your council tax

Council Tax carer's discount

What is it?

If there are less than two people living in, *or* "treated as living in", a property, then you may qualify for a discount on your council tax.

Who is it for?

You can be treated as *not* living in the property if you meet the following criteria:

- living in the same house as the person being cared for; and

- providing care for at least 35 hours a week; and

- not the partner or parent (if the disabled person is under 18) of the person needing care (which of course means foster carers are eligible); and

- caring for somebody entitled to the high rate of the care component of Disability Living Allowance.

How to claim

Either request a form from your local council or use the sample letter in Appendix 3.

Council Tax disability reduction

What is it?
A disability reduction will drop your council tax down one band.

Who is it for?
To be eligible for the disability reduction in your council tax, the property must have one of the following features:

- a room (but not bathroom, kitchen or lavatory) used predominantly by the disabled person; or

- an additional bathroom or kitchen necessary for meeting the needs of the disabled person; or

- sufficient floor space to permit the use of a wheelchair.

The feature must be of major importance to the disabled person's well-being.

How to claim
Either request a form from your local council or use the sample letter in Appendix 2.

Foster care for a looked after child

This chapter covers the situation in which a looked after child has been placed with you by the local authority in a formal fostering arrangement under s23 of the Children Act 1989.

It also covers **kinship or "family and friends" care**, which means the child is looked after and the local authority arranges for the child to be fostered by extended family members or close friends of the family, who have been approved as foster carers by the local authority.

(For informal kinship care, when the child is not a "looked after" child, see Chapter 3.)

In general, the implications of formal foster care for your benefits are straightforward. You cannot claim any extra benefit because of having a foster child in your family, but the payments (allowances and/or fees) you receive for fostering do not count as income.

Can you claim benefits for the fostered child?

In terms of benefits, foster children are not classed as a member of your family if they are placed with you under s23 of the Children Act 1989 and you are being paid an allowance out of public funding – so you cannot include them in any claim for benefits. The fostering allowance is intended to cover the cost of looking after the child.

Therefore, you will not get any *extra* Income Support, Jobseeker's Allowance, Housing Benefit and Council Tax Benefit for your foster child.

Child Benefit

You cannot claim Child Benefit either. You do not have to be the biological mother or father to claim benefit for a child who is living with you – but Child Benefit is not payable:

- if the child is provided with or placed in accommodation; and

- you are paid an allowance for maintenance or accommodation or both out of public or local funds.

This, of course, is the case if you are fostering a looked after child.

Child Tax Credit

The child does not count as a member of your family for Child Tax Credit purposes. (You may still be eligible for Child Tax Credit if you have your own dependent children.)

Working Tax Credit

The child does not count as a member of your family for Working Tax Credit purposes.

To claim Working Tax Credit, you will have to have your own dependent children (or meet one of the other criteria mentioned in the basic rules for Working Tax Credit in Chapter 1).

Do foster payments count as income?

No – generally speaking, fostering payments are not taken into account when working out your income. So if you are claiming means-tested benefits, the allowances and fees you get for fostering will not reduce the amount of benefit you get. Unless you are earning a considerable amount from fostering, you will not have to pay tax on it and you will still be eligible to claim tax credits.

Income Support, Employment and Support Allowance, Jobseeker's Allowance, Housing Benefit, Council Tax Benefit and Pension Credit

These are all means-tested benefits; the more income you have, the less benefits you get. However, for foster carers receiving these benefits, any fostering payments are disregarded. In other words, you will still receive your full entitlement irrespective of the amount of your fostering payments.

Employment and Support Allowance (or Incapacity Benefit) and Carer's Allowance

Normally people cannot claim Employment and Support Allowance (or Incapacity Benefit) if they earn more than £92 a week; and they cannot claim Carer's Allowance if they earn more than £95 a week. However, payments made to foster carers for children placed under s23 of the Children Act 1989 have been specifically disregarded. Therefore, your fostering payments should not affect any entitlement to Employment and Support Allowance, Incapacity Benefit (although check out below on the rules for paid work) or Carer's Allowance.

Child Tax Credit and Working Tax Credit

For these tax credits, any payments received through fostering are ignored as income so long as the payments qualify for tax relief. The tax relief for foster carers is currently £10,000 a year plus £250 a week for each child aged 11 and over and £200 a week for each child aged under 11. If your fostering payments are less than that individual limit, you will be exempt from tax. That will mean that your fostering payments are effectively nil and do not count as earnings when working out your entitlement to Working Tax Credit and Child Tax Credit.

If your income from fostering payments is above the individual limit, you will be taxed on that income (above the individual limit) and that amount will count as earnings when working out your entitlement to Working Tax Credit and Child Tax Credit.

Does fostering count as "work" when claiming benefits?

There are some benefits which you can claim only if you (or your partner) are working, and others that you cannot claim if you (or your partner) are working. Depending on what you are claiming, fostering may or may not be seen as "work" – but in general you will find that the rules work in your favour.

The following benefits *may* be affected by work:

- Income Support

- Jobseeker's Allowance

- Working Tax Credit

- Employment and Support Allowance or Incapacity Benefit

- Carer's Allowance

Income Support, Employment and Support Allowance and Jobseeker's Allowance

People in full-time paid work are excluded from claiming these benefits. Full-time work means 16 hours a week or more for yourself, if you are claiming, and 24 hours a week or more for your partner. However, the regulations make it clear that fostering is *not* to be treated as paid work irrespective of the number of hours involved.

Sickness and incapacity benefits

The rules become more complicated if you are claiming Income Support (on the grounds of sickness) or Incapacity Benefit. One of the conditions for claiming these benefits is that you are incapable of work.

The *Decision Makers' Guide* (a tool used by the Department for Work and Pensions to interpret the law) attempts to provide direction to this rather complicated issue of whether fostering counts as work. It states that if you are attending to personal care, supervision or education of children, then fostering *will* be treated as work. It seems highly likely that you will be providing that level of service and your entitlement to Employment and Support Allowance, Incapacity Benefit and/or Income Support (on the grounds of sickness) could be affected. It goes on to state that if you are fostering a child with a disability, you will be paid an extra allowance which will be regarded as being for work over and above the normal domestic duties.

If the number of hours spent on fostering work is less than 16 a week, it is possible to remain on benefits under what is called "permitted work". But if you spend more than 16 hours a week on fostering work, your benefits may be affected.

However, if you are one of a couple and can show that your partner does the fostering duties, you may find a way around this disqualification.

For Employment and Support Allowance claimants, the rules make it clear that fostering should **not** be seen as work.

If you are a foster carer in receipt of Employment and Support Allowance, Incapacity Benefit or Income Support (on the grounds of sickness), seek individual assistance from your fostering agency.

Jobseeker's Allowance

By claiming Jobseeker's Allowance you are saying that you are available for, and actively seeking, work. You may need to show that the presence of a foster child in your house does not affect your ability to look for work. For example, you may need to show that you could make adequate childcare arrangements.

Working Tax Credit

To be able to claim Working Tax Credit you have to be in paid work of at least 16 hours a week. HM Revenue & Customs will accept that fostering counts as paid work, and will accept the number of hours you state on the claim form.

> **Tax Credit Technical Manual 02404 states that:**
>
> '(foster carers) will still be treated as being in qualifying remunerative work and the number of working hours declared on the form should be accepted'.

If you are claiming Working Tax Credit, you should notify the Tax Credits Office if you do not have a foster child living with you (even if you are paid a retainer) as it is possible that you will not be treated as being in paid work during that period.

Carer's Allowance

Under Carer's Allowance rules there is no limit on the number of hours you can work. The fact that you are fostering full-time will make no difference to your entitlement to Carer's Allowance.

Other effects of fostering on benefits

Jobseeker's Allowance and Income Support

If you are a single person (without employment) without a disability, no children and are not a carer, then you will have to claim Jobseeker's Allowance and not Income Support. This means "signing on" every fortnight to prove that you are actively seeking work.

However, the presence of a foster child in your household will mean that you are treated as a single parent (although the child cannot count as a member of your family) and can claim Income Support instead.

This means you will not have to "sign on" as unemployed and prove to the Job Centre that you are actively seeking work. You will, of course, have to satisfy all the other eligibility criteria for Income Support (see Chapter 1). You can be treated as available for work for up to eight weeks if you are looking after a child under 16 because the parent is ill.

Jobseeker's Allowance and couples

Couples without children usually have to make a joint claim for Jobseeker's Allowance – that means that both partners will have to be available for, and actively seeking, work. However, claimants who are fostering a looked after child will be treated as responsible for that child (although extra benefit will not be paid), and only one member of the couple will have to make a claim for Jobseeker's Allowance.

Housing Benefit

People who rent accommodation from a private landlord sometimes have restrictions attached to their claim for Housing Benefit. The local council may restrict the amount of Housing Benefit you receive if they consider that you are under-occupying your property, that is, you have a larger property than you need for the number of people in your household.

If this applies to you, a foster child (even though he or she does not count as a member of your family) should count as another occupier in the property and should reduce the restriction.

However, some local councils may take a different view. The *Housing Benefit Guidance Manual* (which contains guidance from the Department for Work & Pensions) states that foster children should *not* count as an occupier as to do otherwise would result in double provision as foster carers are paid to accommodate children. This interpretation of the law is debatable as the law does not differentiate between a resident's own children and foster children. If the local council does not agree to reduce the restriction, you may need to appeal. For help with this, contact the Citizens Advice Bureau or your social worker.

There is an element in the Housing Benefit and Council Tax Benefit schemes called discretionary housing payments. If your award of Housing Benefit is not enough to cover your rent (or your Council Tax Benefit is not enough to cover your council tax), it is possible to get a payment to meet some, or all, of the shortfall. You have to apply to the local authority that administers your Housing Benefit and Council Tax Benefit. However, councils do not have to make these payments and there is no right of appeal against refusal. It is at the discretion of the local council as to whether they treat the fostering allowance as a source of income and reduce your discretionary housing payment accordingly. You need to check with your local council.

CASE STUDY: **FOSTER CARE FOR A LOOKED AFTER CHILD**

Bob is an approved foster carer. He is single and does not have any children. The local authority place Aaron (aged five) with him, under s23, and Bob is paid a fostering allowance. Bob also gets Jobseeker's Allowance of £64.30 a week as well as Housing Benefit and Council Tax Benefit. He cannot get any extra benefits for Aaron as it is a foster placement under s23.

Bob has three choices with his benefits:

1. He can continue on Jobseeker's Allowance – payment of the fostering allowance will not affect his Jobseeker's Allowance, Housing Benefit or Council Tax Benefit*; or

2. He can claim Income Support instead of Jobseeker's Allowance (on the grounds of being a foster carer). The amount he receives will be exactly the same but he will not have to "sign on" as unemployed; or

3. He can choose to be considered as self-employed and claim Working Tax Credit instead as long as he is aged at least 25 and is working at least 30 hours a week. The fostering allowance will not count as an income and he will get £51.25 a week in Working Tax Credit (the maximum amount payable) on top of the fostering allowance.

Bob lives in a two-bedroom privately-rented flat. There is a restriction on his Housing Benefit (as he only requires one bedroom). Once Aaron moves in, Bob is no longer under-occupying the house and the Housing Benefit restriction should be lifted.

* However, some local authorities may not approve of Bob claiming Jobseeker's Allowance while he is fostering.

CASE STUDY: **KINSHIP CARE FOR A LOOKED AFTER CHILD**

Lauren and her eight-year-old daughter live in a three-bedroom property. She claims Income Support as a single parent. Her nine-year-old nephew, Daniel, comes to live with her. Daniel is a looked after child, placed under s23.

Lauren cannot claim Child Benefit or Child Tax Credit for Daniel as he is a looked after child (although she can receive those benefits for her daughter). Lauren has two choices:

1. She can continue on Income Support as a single parent. The money she receives from the local authority for looking after Daniel is disregarded as income; her Income Support remains the same; or

2. She can be treated as being self-employed and claim Working Tax Credit. As her formal kinship care payments will be below her individual limit, her taxable income will be nil and she will get full Working Tax Credit of £87.02 a week currently. (Lauren receives more than Bob in the previous case study because she is a single parent.)

Lauren's Housing Benefit has been restricted as she and her daughter only need two bedrooms. When Daniel comes to live with them, they are still treated as under-occupying the accommodation as the rules allow only one bedroom for two children under 10. The fact that Daniel has his own room is irrelevant.

BENEFITS SNAPSHOT:
FOSTERING AND KINSHIP CARE
OF A LOOKED AFTER CHILD

	Can you claim extra for the child?	Do payments count as income?	Does fostering count as work?
Child Benefit	No	–	–
Income Support	No	No	No*
Housing Benefit	No	No	–
Council Tax Benefit	No	No	–
Jobseeker's Allowance	No	No	No
Council tax discounts	Yes (if child has disability)	–	–
Child Tax Credit	No	No	–
Working Tax Credit	–	No	Yes
Incapacity Benefit or Employment & Support Allowance	No	No	No*
Carer's Allowance	No	No	No
Pension Credit	No	No	–

* For people claiming Income Support (by sending in sickness certificates) or Incapacity Benefit, there remains some dispute.

Kinship care for a "non-looked after" child

This chapter is for you if you are caring for a child and are paid an allowance under s17 of the Children Act 1989. For example, if:

- the child is not a looked after child under the care of the local authority but is living with you (a relative or close friend) and the local authority provides some financial support; or

- the child is not provided with accommodation by the local authority because he or she lives at home (e.g. in the case of day care and respite fostering).

Can you claim benefits for the child?

Benefit is often refused for children who are fostered as payments are being made from elsewhere. If the child is not looked after by the local authority then, often, benefits can be claimed for that child.

Child Benefit
You can claim this if you have a child living with you. You do not have to be the biological mother or father. For informal kinship care, the child is not provided

with or placed in accommodation by the local authority and so Child Benefit should be payable.

Guardian's Allowance
If you receive Child Benefit, then you may also be able to claim Guardian's Allowance if both the child's parents have died or one is dead and the other is detained in prison or in hospital by order of a court or no-one knows where he or she is.

Income Support and Jobseeker's Allowance
These can only be claimed for a child if you are responsible for a child and living in the same household as the child.

For informal kinship care, the child should count as a member of your household (as the child is not placed under s23) and you may be able to claim extra benefit for the child. However, this will only apply if you were continuously in receipt of Income Support or Jobseeker's Allowance (with a dependent child included) since before April 2004. New claimants of these benefits cannot claim for any children (whether your own or those under informal kinship care).

Housing Benefit and Council Tax Benefit
You can claim extra Housing Benefit and Council Tax Benefit for a child if you are responsible for a child and live in the same household as the child. In informal kinship care, you can claim extra Housing Benefit and Council Tax Benefit for the child.

Child Tax Credit
People who cannot claim extra Income Support or Jobseeker's Allowance for a child in informal kinship care can claim Child Tax Credit.

Incapacity Benefit, Employment and Support Allowance, Pension Credit and Carer's Allowance
You cannot include children in any claim for these benefits.

Do payments count as income?

In informal kinship care, the financial support you receive does not generally count as an income for most benefits.

Income Support, Jobseeker's Allowance, Employment and Support Allowance, Housing Benefit, Council Tax Benefit

Payments made to informal kinship carers are usually made through s17 of the Children Act 1989 and – like other fostering allowances – should not count as income when you are claiming benefits. In other words, you will still receive your full entitlement to the benefits above, irrespective of the financial assistance you receive.

Tax Credits

Any payments received through informal kinship care are ignored as income for Child Tax Credit and Working Tax Credit, as payments from the local authority under s17 are not taxable.

Employment and Support Allowance, Incapacity Benefit and Carer's Allowance

You cannot claim Employment and Support Allowance (contribution-based), Incapacity Benefit or Carer's Allowance if you earn above a certain amount (currently £95 a week for Carer's Allowance and £92 for Incapacity Benefit or Employment and Support Allowance). It is debateable whether informal kinship care should be treated as work (as you do not receive any reward element in your payments). However, if the Department for Work & Pensions do treat it as work, then any payments over £92 or £95 will affect your entitlement to Employment and Support Allowance, Incapacity Benefit or Carer's Allowance.

Pension Credit

Only income that is specified in the rules can affect your Pension Credit. As s17 payments are not included in the rules, they should be ignored.

Does kinship care count as work?

Informal kinship care should not count as work and there are three reasons for this: there is no reward element in the payment that you receive; looking after your children does not usually count as work (informal kinship care children will often count as your own children for benefits purposes); and you are not formally approved by the local authority as a foster carer.

Income Support, Employment and Support Allowance and Incapacity Benefit

The rules may be more complicated if you are an informal kinship carer claiming Income Support (on the grounds of sickness), Incapacity Benefit or Employment and Support Allowance. One of the conditions of entitlement is that you are incapable of work. It is possible to undertake certain paid work and remain in receipt of these benefits. The care of relatives is one of the kinds of work that is allowable. Relatives have been defined as brother, sister, nephew, niece or grandchild. If your kinship care child is one of those relatives, then it should not count as work. If the kinship care child is not one of those relatives, the work that you are undertaking may be treated as work and affect your Incapacity Benefit, Income Support or Employment and Support Allowance.

For those claiming Employment and Support Allowance, it may be possible to argue that the care of a person not normally a member of your household should not be treated as work.

If you are one of a couple and can show that your partner does the fostering duties you may find a way around this disqualification.

If you are a kinship carer claiming benefit by sending in medical certificates, seek individual assistance.

Jobseeker's Allowance

By claiming Jobseeker's Allowance you are saying that you are available for, and actively seeking, work. You may need to show that having the child in your home does not affect your ability to look for work.

Working Tax Credit

Informal kinship care should not count as paid work as the children have not been placed under s23. To qualify for Working Tax Credit you will have to have other employment.

Carer's Allowance

There is no limit on the number of hours you can work and still be eligible for Carer's Allowance.

Other effects of kinship care on benefits

Jobseeker's Allowance/Income Support

If you are a single person (without employment) without a disability, no children and are not a carer, then you have to claim Jobseeker's Allowance and not Income Support. This means that you have to "sign on" every fortnight and prove that you are actively seeking work. However, the presence of a kinship care child *under the age of 12* in your household will mean that you are treated as a single parent (although the child cannot count as a member of your family) and you can claim Income Support instead. This means you will not have to "sign on" as unemployed and prove to the Job Centre that you are actively seeking work. You will, of course, have to satisfy all the other eligibility criteria for Income Support (see p. 10).

Housing Benefit

People who rent accommodation from a private landlord may have restrictions attached to their claim for Housing Benefit. This is particularly relevant if they are assessed as under-occupying that property; that is, there are fewer people living in the property than the rules allow. If this applies to you, the local council may restrict the amount of Housing Benefit you receive. However, the presence of a child should count as another occupier in the property and the restriction should be lifted.

You should note, though, that the Housing Benefit Guidance Manual used by local councils does not share this interpretation so you may run up against difficulties. If necessary, seek help from the Citizens Advice Bureau or your social worker.

Discretionary housing payments

There is an element in the Housing Benefit and Council Tax Benefit schemes called discretionary housing payments. If your award of Housing Benefit is not enough to cover your rent (or your award of Council Tax Benefit is not enough to cover your council tax), it is possible to get a payment to meet some, or all, of the shortfall. You need to apply to the local authority that administers your Housing Benefit or Council Tax Benefit. However, payments of discretionary housing payments are not compulsory and there is no right of appeal against refusal. It is up to the local council to decide whether they will treat the fostering allowance as a source of income and reduce your discretionary housing payment. You need to check with your local council.

CASE STUDY: **KINSHIP CARE OF A NON-LOOKED AFTER CHILD**

Jack and Elsie are both aged 65. They are looking after their granddaughter, Jasmine (who is not a looked after child), as informal kinship carers.

Jasmine counts as a member of their household and so they can claim Child Benefit and Child Tax Credit and extra Housing Benefit and Council Tax Benefit for her. The financial assistance they receive does not count as income and so will not affect any of their means-tested benefits – Pension Credit, Housing Benefit, Council Tax Benefit or Child Tax Credit.

BENEFITS SNAPSHOT:
KINSHIP CARE OF
NON-LOOKED AFTER CHILD

	Can you claim extra for the child?	Do payments count as income?	Does fostering count as work?
Child Benefit	Yes	–	–
Income Support	Yes*	No	**
Housing Benefit	Yes	No	–
Council Tax Benefit	Yes	No	–
Jobseeker's Allowance	Yes*	No	**
Council tax discounts	Yes (if child has disability)	–	–
Child Tax Credit	Yes	No	–
Working Tax Credit	–	No	No
Incapacity Benefit or Employment & Support Allowance	No	**	**
Carer's Allowance	No	**	**
Pension Credit	No	No	–

* N.B.: but only if you have been continuously in receipt of this benefit since April 2004 with a child included.

** The law is uncertain on whether kinship care of non-looked after children counts as work.

Day care and respite care/ short breaks

4

Day care fostering

A small number of children require planned day foster care. They don't need to sleep at the foster home but do need the care and attention of a foster carer during the day, perhaps because they find attending school difficult or their parent needs extra help during the day.

Respite care/short breaks

Some foster carers provide respite care or short breaks for children whose parents need a bit of help. For instance, parents who have a child with a disability may be offered some respite care for their child, to give them much-needed time to catch up with other things, spend time with their other children or have a rest. For example, a foster carer or family might provide respite care for a child for one weekend every month.

These children are not looked after children.

FOR BOTH DAY CARE AND RESPITE CARE

Can you claim benefits for the child?

The effect on the foster carer benefits is minimal. The child should not be included in any benefits you receive.

Child Benefit is not payable as the child is not living with you.

Income Support, Jobseeker's Allowance, Housing Benefit, Council Tax Benefit are not payable for the child because you are not living in the same household as the child.

Child Tax Credit and Working Tax Credit are not payable for the child because you are not responsible for the child.

Does payment count as income?

Generally, day care fostering and respite care are both funded under s17 of the Children Act 1989. All s17 payments are ignored as income for all means-tested benefits and tax credits (Income Support, Jobseeker's Allowance, Housing Benefit, Council Tax Benefit, Child Tax Credit, Working Tax Credit and Pension Credit). If you are not sure under which budget you are paid, check with your social worker.

DAY CARE

Does day care fostering count as work?

As a day care foster carer, you are likely to be paid a fixed hourly rate. This should count as being in paid work. If you work for 16 hours a week or more, then Income Support and Jobseeker's Allowance could be affected.

If the earnings are above £95 a week, it will affect Carer's Allowance.

If the earnings are above £92 a week, it will affect Incapacity Benefit, Employment and Support Allowance or Income Support (claiming on the grounds of sickness). The exemptions mentioned elsewhere (work as a foster carer is disregarded if the child is placed under s23) do not apply for day care foster workers as the child lives with someone else. If you claim Incapacity Benefit, Employment and Support Allowance and/or Income Support (on the grounds of sickness) it would be advisable to get the permission of the Department for Work & Pensions before you undertake any day care fostering as it could impact on the benefit.

If you are working 16 hours or more each week, you may be eligible to claim Working Tax Credit.

Other effects of day care fostering

Day care fostering may also affect two benefits in different ways.

To qualify for Jobseeker's Allowance you must be available for, and actively seeking, work. By providing a day care fostering service, you may be treated as unavailable for, and not actively seeking, work. If the decision-maker does not believe you are available for and seeking work, you may be refused Jobseeker's Allowance.

If you are in any doubt about whether your day care service affects your Jobseeker's Allowance, you need to discuss it with your social worker and the Job Centre immediately.

RESPITE CARE/SHORT BREAKS

Does respite fostering count as work?

As a respite carer you are likely to be paid a fixed hourly rate. This should count as being in remunerative work. If you do 16 hours a week or more, it could affect your entitlement to Income Support and Jobseeker's Allowance.

If the earnings are above £95 a week, it will affect Carer's Allowance.

If the earnings are above £92 a week, it will affect Incapacity Benefit, Employment and Support Allowance or Income Support (claiming on the grounds of sickness). The exemptions mentioned elsewhere (work as a foster carer is disregarded if the child is placed under s23) do not apply for respite foster carers as the child lives with someone else. If you claim Incapacity Benefit, Employment and Support Allowance and/or Income Support (on the grounds of sickness) it would be advisable to get the permission of the Department for Work & Pensions before you undertake any work as it could impact on the benefit.

If you are working 16 hours or more each week, you may be eligible to claim Working Tax Credit.

Other effects of respite fostering

Respite fostering may potentially affect just one benefit. To qualify for Jobseeker's Allowance, you must satisfy the labour market conditions, i.e. be available for, and actively seeking, work. By providing a respite fostering service, you may be treated as unavailable for, and not actively seeking, work during the time you are providing respite. If the decision-maker does not believe you are available for and seeking work, you may be refused Jobseeker's Allowance.

If you are in any doubt about this, discuss it with your social worker and the Job Centre immediately.

CASE STUDY: **DAY CARE**

Terry and Diane provide day care services four days a week. The effect on their benefits is minimal. They cannot get Child Benefit or Child Tax Credit for any of the children because they do not live with them. They currently receive Housing Benefit and Council Tax Benefit. The day care should not affect those benefits as all s17 payments are disregarded. However, they should be treated as being in work and therefore would qualify for Working Tax Credit.

CASE STUDY: **RESPITE CARE**

Bev provides respite care to Kieran for one weekend every month. She also works at the local shop for 15 hours a week. She will not qualify for Working Tax Credit if the number of hours spent working on respite average less than 16 a week. However, the respite hours could be added to her shop work hours, which would take her weekly hours to over 16 and she would then be able to claim Working Tax Credit.

BENEFITS SNAPSHOT:
DAY CARE AND RESPITE CARE
(IF FUNDED UNDER SECTION 17)

	Can you claim extra for the child?	Do payments count as income?	Does fostering count as work?
Child Benefit	No	–	–
Income Support	No	No	Yes
Housing Benefit	No	No	–
Council Tax Benefit	No	No	–
Jobseeker's Allowance	No	No	Yes
Council tax discounts	No	–	–
Child Tax Credit	No	No	–
Working Tax Credit	–	No	If over 16 hours per week
Incapacity Benefit or Employment & Support Allowance	No	?	If over £92 per week
Carer's Allowance	No	No	If over £95 per week
Pension Credit	No	No	–

Where a question mark appears (?) there is some doubt as this may depend on circumstances. Contact your social worker to have this checked out for you.

Residence orders and special guardianship

5

This chapter covers residence orders and special guardianship.

- **Residence orders** are court orders stating where and with whom a child shall live. It is often informal kinship or "family and friends" carers who take out a residence order.

- **Special guardianship** is a court order intended to provide legal permanence for children in England and Wales who cannot live with their birth families. The child will no longer be the responsibility of the local authority but in some cases the special guardian, if he or she has been the foster carer of the child, continues to receive some payment for fostering, in addition to the maintenance element of the fostering payment, for some time after the order is made.

Can you claim benefits for the child?

As the child is not looked after by the local authority, you should be able to claim Child Benefit and Child Tax Credit for the child.

Income Support and Jobseeker's Allowance should be payable for the child as long as you were continuously in receipt of those benefits since April 2004 and had a child included in the claim. New claimants do not get extra for their children.

For Housing Benefit and Council Tax Benefit, the child can count as a member of your household.

Does payment count as income?

If you are paid a residence order or special guardianship allowance for looking after a child, the benefit situation is quite different from those in the previous chapters.

For Income Support and Jobseeker's Allowance (if you are also being paid Child Tax Credit) the whole of the allowance is ignored.

For Income Support and Jobseeker's Allowance (if you are not being paid Child Tax Credit) and Housing Benefit and Council Tax Benefit the first £56.11 per child (or £107.35 if disabled) of the allowance counts as income and will affect these benefits. The remainder will be ignored.

Residence order allowances are taken into account in full for Housing Benefit and Council Tax Benefit.

For Pension Credit, the whole of the allowance is ignored.

For Child Tax Credit and Working Tax Credit, the whole of the allowance is ignored.

Does it count as work?

As the child counts as a member of your household for all benefits, then the child caring work you are doing should not count as work. However, this might still be subject to individual local decisions by the Department for Work and Pensions.

CASE STUDY: **SPECIAL GUARDIANSHIP**

Melanie and Dave are foster carers for Connor. They apply for and are awarded special guardianship. As Connor is no longer a looked after child, Melanie and Dave can apply for Child Benefit and Child Tax Credit for him. However, they should be advised that their Working Tax Credit could be affected as their caring for Connor may not be classed as work. They should notify the Tax Credit Office.

BENEFITS SNAPSHOT:
RESIDENCE ORDERS AND
SPECIAL GUARDIANSHIP ALLOWANCES

	Can you claim extra for the child?	Do payments count as income?	Does fostering count as work?
Child Benefit	Yes	–	–
Income Support	Not for new claims	No*	No
Housing Benefit	Yes	Yes**	–
Council Tax Benefit	Yes	Yes**	–
Jobseeker's Allowance	Not for new claims	No*	No
Council tax discounts	Yes, if child has disability	–	–
Child Tax Credit	Yes	No	–
Working Tax Credit	–	No	No
Incapacity Benefit or Employment & Support Allowance	No	?	No
Carer's Allowance	No	No	No
Pension Credit	No	No	–

Where a question mark appears (?) there is some doubt. Contact your social worker to have this checked out for you.

* No, if you receive Child Tax Credit. Otherwise, the first £56.11 per child (or £107.35 if disabled) counts.

** For special guardianship allowances, the first £56.11 per child (or £107.35 if disabled) counts.

Parent & baby placements

A parent and baby placement is where a parent and child have been placed with you by the local authority under s23 (in England and Wales). The child or the parent (who in some cases will also be a child under 16) or both will be under a care order or accommodated by the local authority. They stay with you full-time but generally for a fixed period. You are recompensed by the local authority through a fostering allowance.

Below, we look only at the benefits that affect the foster carer, not the parent(s) – although mention is made of those only to show the impact on the carer's benefits.

Can you claim benefits for the fostered child?

Child Benefit
Child Benefit is not payable in the following situation:

- if the child is provided with or placed in accommodation; and

- you are paid an allowance for maintenance or accommodation or both out of public or local funds.

Both of these factors need to apply for Child Benefit *not* to be payable. It is probable that the baby is under the care of the local authority and that a fostering allowance is paid out of public or local funds. Therefore, Child Benefit will not be payable. If you are not sure, check with your social worker.

Income Support and Jobseeker's Allowance

These can only be claimed for a child if you are responsible for a child and living in the same household as the child. However, you will not be treated as living in the same household if the child is fostered by you under s23 of the Children Act 1989. Most foster children are placed under s23. If this is the case for you, the child cannot count as a member of your family.

Housing Benefit and Council Tax Benefit

The rules for these benefits are similar to the rules for Income Support. You can only claim them for a child if you are responsible for a child and live in the same household as the child.

However, you will not be treated as living in the same household if the child is fostered by you under s23 of the Children Act 1989. Therefore the child cannot count as a member of your family.

Child Tax Credit and Working Tax Credit

Foster children do not count as a member of your family for Child Tax Credit purposes where the child is placed with you and is funded under s23 of the Children Act 1989 or other public funding. You may still be eligible for Child Tax Credit if you have your own dependent children.

To be eligible for Working Tax Credit you will also have to have your own dependent children (or fit one of the other criteria mentioned in Chapter 1).

Employment and Support Allowance, Incapacity Benefit and Carer's Allowance
You cannot claim extra for children.

Pension Credit
You cannot claim extra for children.

Do payments count as income?

Income Support, Jobseeker's Allowance, Housing Benefit, Council Tax Benefit
The above are means-tested benefits; the more income you have, the less you receive in benefits. However, any payments you receive for fostering should not count as income as far as these benefits are concerned. In other words, you will still receive your full entitlement irrespective of your fostering allowance.

Child Tax Credit and Working Tax Credit
Any payments you receive through fostering are ignored as income for tax credits so long as the payments qualify for tax relief.

If your fostering payments are less than an individual limit (see page 21) you will be exempt from tax. That will mean that your fostering payments will not count as earnings as far as Working Tax Credit is concerned.

If your income from fostering payments is above the limit, you will be taxed on that income (above the individual limit) and it will count as earnings towards Working Tax Credit.

Employment and Support Allowance, Incapacity Benefit and Carer's Allowance

You cannot normally claim Employment and Support Allowance or Incapacity Benefit if you earn more than £92 a week and you cannot normally claim Carer's Allowance if you earn more than £95 a week. However, fostering payments made under s23 of the Children Act 1989 are disregarded. So your income from fostering should not affect any entitlement to these benefits (although fostering may be seen as paid work – see below).

Pension Credit

A fostering allowance does not count as income for Pension Credit, so its value is ignored.

Does fostering count as work when claiming benefits?

Income Support and Jobseeker's Allowance

You cannot claim Income Support or Jobseeker's Allowance if you are in full-time paid work. (Full-time work means 16 hours or more for yourself and 24 hours or more for your partner.) However, the regulations make it clear that foster carers are not to be treated as doing paid work, irrespective of the number of hours involved.

By claiming Jobseeker's Allowance you are saying that you are available for, and actively seeking, work. You may need to show that the presence of a foster child in your house does not affect your ability to look for work, for example, that you have adequate childcare arrangements in place.

Incapacity Benefit and Income Support (on the grounds of sickness)

The rules may be more complicated if you are claiming Employment and Support Allowance, Incapacity Benefit or Income Support on the grounds of sickness (rather than as a single parent or carer). To claim these benefits, you must be incapable of work. It is possible to undertake certain paid work and continue on Incapacity Benefit. Domestic work in your own home is one of the kinds of work that is allowable.

The Decision Makers' Guide (issued by the Department for Work & Pensions) attempts to provide direction to this complicated issue of whether fostering counts as work. (*The Decision Makers' Guide* is exactly that: a guide to the law, *not* the law itself. However, decision-makers do take it into account.) It states that looking after other people's children should be considered within the definition of work. If attending to personal care, supervision or education of children takes place, then fostering will be treated as work. It seems highly likely that you will be providing that level of service and your entitlement to Incapacity Benefit or Income Support (claiming on grounds of sickness) could be affected. It goes on to state that if you are fostering a child with a disability, you will be paid an extra allowance which will be regarded as being for work over and above the normal domestic duties.

If you are one of a couple and can show that your partner does the fostering duties, you may find a way around this disqualification.

If you are claiming Employment and Support Allowance, the rules now make it clear that fostering should not be seen as work.

If you are a foster carer claiming Incapacity Benefit or Income Support on the grounds of sickness, please seek individual assistance.

Working Tax Credit

To be able to claim Working Tax Credit, you have to be in paid work of at least 16 hours a week. There is good news in that fostering is generally taken as remunerative work.

> **Tax Credit Technical Manual 02404 states that:**
>
> '(foster carers) will still be treated as being in qualifying remunerative work and the number of working hours declared on the form should be accepted'.

Carer's Allowance

There is no limit on the number of hours you can work and still be eligible for Carer's Allowance.

Other effects of placements on benefits

If you are a single person (without employment) without a disability, no children and not a carer, then you will have to claim Jobseeker's Allowance and not Income Support. This means that you will have to "sign on" every fortnight and prove that you are actively seeking work.

Having a foster child under the age of 16 in your household will mean that you are treated as a single parent (although the child cannot count as a member of your family) and can claim Income Support instead. This means you do not have to "sign on" as unemployed and prove to the Job Centre that you are actively seeking work. You will, of course, have to satisfy all the other eligibility criteria for Income Support (see Chapter 1).

Couples without children normally have to make a joint claim for Jobseeker's Allowance – that means that both partners will have to be available for, and actively seeking, work. But if you are looking after a child for the local authority, under s23 of the Children Act 1989, you will be treated as responsible for that child. You and your partner will not have to make a joint claim for Jobseeker's Allowance.

Income Support, Jobseeker's Allowance, Employment and Support Allowance and Pension Credit can help pay towards your housing costs if there is still a mortgage on the property. Housing Benefit can help pay towards your rent. However, the presence of a non-dependant (the baby's parent) in the property means that a deduction will be made from any housing costs that you get in your Income Support, Jobseeker's Allowance, Pension Credit and Housing Benefit. No deduction will be made, though, in the following circumstances:

- where you are blind or receiving the care component of Disability Living Allowance or Attendance Allowance;

- where the non-dependant is 16 or 17 years old;

- where the non-dependant is under 25 and getting Income Support or income-based Jobseeker's Allowance;

- where the non-dependant has a home elsewhere;

- where the non-dependant is a full-time student.

If the non-dependant fits into any of the criteria above, for instance, if they still have a home elsewhere, then their presence in your house should not affect your housing costs. Otherwise, the deduction is a set amount based on the non-dependant's income. The deduction ranges from £7.40 a week up to £47.75 a week.

People who rent accommodation from a private landlord may have restrictions attached to their claim for Housing Benefit. This is particularly relevant if they are assessed as under-occupying that property; that is, there are fewer people living in the property than the rules allow. If this applies to you, the local council may restrict the amount of Housing Benefit you receive. However, the presence of a parent and baby placement (even though they do not count as a member of your family) should count as occupiers in the property and may mean the restriction is lifted.

There is an element in the Housing Benefit and Council Tax Benefit schemes called discretionary housing payments. If your award of Housing Benefit and

Council Tax Benefit is not enough to cover your rent and council tax, it is possible to get a payment to meet some, or all, of the shortfall. You have to apply to the local authority that administers your benefits. However, payments of discretionary housing payments are not compulsory and there is no right of appeal against refusal. Although the fostering payments are ignored in payments of Housing Benefit and Council Tax Benefit, the local council may decide that the fostering payments should count as income and reduce discretionary housing payments accordingly. You need to check with your local council.

The presence of a non-dependant (the baby's parent) in the property means that a deduction will be made from any Council Tax Benefit that you get. However, no deduction will be made in the following circumstances:

● where you are blind or in receipt of the care component of Disability Living Allowance or Attendance Allowance;

● where the non-dependant is 16 or 17 years old;

● where the non-dependant is in receipt of Income Support or income-based Jobseeker's Allowance;

● where the non-dependant has a home elsewhere;

● where the non-dependant is a full-time student or severely mentally impaired.

If the non-dependant fits into any of the criteria above, then their presence in your house should not affect your Council Tax Benefit. Otherwise, the deduction is a set amount based on the non-dependant's income. The deduction ranges from £2.30 a week up to £6.95 a week.

CASE STUDY: **PARENT AND BABY PLACEMENTS**

Julie is a single parent with a seven-year-old daughter, Megan. She has a parent and baby placement – Georgina, who is 23 years old, and her baby son, who is a looked after child. Georgina has cerebral palsy.

Julie claims Housing Benefit and Council Tax Benefit. The fostering payment she receives will not count as income and no non-dependant deductions will be made from her benefits as Georgina gets Income Support in her own right.

Julie can decide whether to continue getting Income Support or to be classed as self-employed and claim Working Tax Credit. She would get £87.02 on Working Tax Credit but would have to pay some extra rent and council tax and would no longer get free prescriptions.

BENEFITS SNAPSHOT:
PARENT AND BABY PLACEMENTS

	Can you claim extra for the child?	Do payments count as income?	Does fostering count as work?
Child Benefit	No	–	–
Income Support	No	No*	No**
Housing Benefit	No	No*	–
Council Tax Benefit	No	No*	–
Jobseeker's Allowance	No	No	No
Council tax discounts	Yes	–	–
Child Tax Credit	No	No	–
Working Tax Credit	–	No	Yes
Incapacity Benefit or Employment & Support Allowance	No	No	No**
Carer's Allowance	No	No	No
Pension Credit	No	No*	–

* The presence of a non-dependant in the household may affect these benefits.

** For people claiming Income Support (by sending in a certificate for sickness) or Incapacity Benefit, there remains some dispute.

Private fostering

Private fostering is a private arrangement in which a parent or parents arrange for their child under 16 (or under 18 and disabled) to live with someone else. This other person is not a parent, a relative, a person with parental responsibility or the local authority, and the period of care is intended to last 28 days or more. The child is not in the care system and the parent or parents pay the carer.

In terms of your benefits, private fostering has the same implications as having a child of your own.

Can you claim benefits for the privately fostered child?

Child Benefit

You can claim Child Benefit if you have a child living with you and you have greater priority over other potential claimants. You do not have to be the biological mother or father. As a private foster carer, you should be able to claim Child Benefit.

If the parents are still receiving Child Benefit themselves, you will not be able to claim Child Benefit until they have stopped getting it. This may take some time. The whole process should be speeded up if the parent co-operates and voluntarily stops their benefit.

Income Support and Jobseeker's Allowance
You will be able to claim extra Income Support or Jobseeker's Allowance for the child only if you have been continuously receiving one of those benefits since before 6 April 2004 with a dependant child included. If you are a new claimant, you cannot claim extra Income Support or Jobseeker's Allowance for any child (whether your own or someone else's).

Housing Benefit and Council Tax Benefit
The child can count as a member of your family for Housing Benefit and Council Tax Benefit purposes.

Child Tax Credit and Working Tax Credit
You should be able to include the child in your claim.

You cannot claim extra Carer's Allowance or Incapacity Benefit or Employment and Support Allowance or Pension Credit for children.

Does a private fostering payment count as income?

The generous rules that apply elsewhere to fostering payments are not totally replicated for private fostering.

Income Support and Jobseeker's Allowance

These are means-tested benefits. If the parent pays you a regular payment to look after their child, it will count as income. Either the whole amount counts (if the agreement was made before 3/3/03) or the first £10 a week will be disregarded (if the agreement was made after 3/3/03). Any payments made to you for your time will count as income unless it is a "payment in kind" (for example, food, fuel, accommodation, clothing). Payments in kind are ignored.

Pension Credit

The whole amount is disregarded.

Housing Benefit and Council Tax Benefit

Regular payments from the parent for the child will be treated as income (although the first £15 a week is disregarded) or capital (if paid irregularly or in lump sums). Any payment made to you for your time will count as income unless it is a "payment in kind" (for example, food, fuel, accommodation, clothing). Payments in kind are ignored.

Working Tax Credit and Child Tax Credit

The rules regarding tax credits are more generous. Any payments for the child made by the child's parent will be disregarded when calculating your tax credits. Any payments made to you for your time will count if you are paying tax on them. Contact the Tax Credit Office on 0845 300 3900.

Carer's Allowance

Private fostering does not count as work for Carer's Allowance, so any payment will not affect Carer's Allowance.

Pension Credit

Any maintenance payments made by the parent of the child will be disregarded when calculating your Pension Credit.

Does private fostering count as work when claiming benefits?

As the child counts as a member of your family for all benefits, private fostering does not count as work and should not affect Income Support, Incapacity Benefit, Employment and Support Allowance, Jobseeker's Allowance or Carer's Allowance. (However, the care of somebody else's child in your household could be seen as work with regards to Income Support, Employment and Support Allowance and Incapacity Benefit.)

Unlike standard fostering, a privately fostered child counts as a member of your family. So private fostering should not be treated as paid work for Working Tax Credit. Therefore, you would have to have other employment in order to qualify for Working Tax Credit.

Other effects of private fostering on benefits

If you are a single person (without employment) without a disability, no children and are not a carer, then you will have to claim Jobseeker's Allowance and not Income Support. This means that you will have to "sign on" every fortnight and prove that you are actively seeking work. Under new rules, having a child under the age of 12 in your household will mean that you are treated as a single parent and can claim Income Support instead. This means you will not have to "sign on" as unemployed and prove to the Job Centre that you are actively seeking work. You will, of course, have to satisfy all the other eligibility criteria for Income Support (see Chapter 1). In future years, this age limit will come down.

Couples without children normally have to make a joint claim for Jobseeker's Allowance – that means that both partners will have to be available for, and actively seeking, work. If you are entitled to Child Benefit you will be treated as responsible for that child – so you and your partner will not have to make a joint claim for Jobseeker's Allowance.

People who rent accommodation from a private landlord may have restrictions attached to their claim for Housing Benefit. This is particularly relevant if they are assessed as under-occupying that property; that is, there are fewer people living in the property than the rules allow. If this applies to you, the local council may restrict the amount of Housing Benefit you receive. However, the presence of a child should count as another occupier in the property and the restriction may be lifted.

There is an element in the Housing Benefit and Council Tax Benefit scheme called discretionary housing payments. If your award of these benefits is not enough to cover your rent and Council Tax, it is possible to get a payment to meet some, or all, of the shortfall. Applications need to be made to the local authority that administers your Housing Benefit and Council Tax Benefit. However, payments of discretionary housing payments are not compulsory and there is no right of appeal against refusal. The local council may decide that the private fostering payments you receive should count as a source of income and reduce your discretionary housing payment accordingly. You need to check with your local council.

CASE STUDY: **PRIVATE FOSTERING**

Wayne's father has to go abroad for a year for business. Rather than disrupt Wayne's schooling, it was agreed that he live with Peter and Jane, the neighbours. Wayne has known them all his life and they have looked after Wayne for various weekends. Wayne has cerebral palsy.

Peter and Jane claim Income Support as Jane is also a carer for her disabled mother. Peter and Jane can claim Child Benefit and Child Tax Credit for Wayne. As Wayne's father gives Peter and Jane £400 a month, this will count as a regular income and their Income Support (as well as their Housing Benefit and Council Tax Benefit) will stop but it will be disregarded as income for their Child Tax Credit – which will be £50 a week.

Peter can claim Carer's Allowance for looking after Wayne (who gets the high rate of the care component of Disability Living Allowance). In the calculation of Council Tax, certain carers can be disregarded although living in the property. Peter and Jane will qualify for the carer's discount of 25%.

BENEFITS SNAPSHOT:
PRIVATE FOSTERING

	Can you claim extra for the child?	Do payments count as income?	Does fostering count as work?
Child Benefit	Yes	–	–
Income Support	Yes*	Yes	No
Housing Benefit	Yes	Yes	–
Council Tax Benefit	Yes	Yes	–
Jobseeker's Allowance	Yes*	Yes	No
Council tax discounts	Yes, if child has a disability	–	–
Child Tax Credit	Yes	No	–
Working Tax Credit	–	No	No
Incapacity Benefit or Employment & Support Allowance	No	No	No**
Carer's Allowance	No	No	No
Pension Credit	No	No	No

* N.B.: But only if you have continuously been in receipt of this benefit since April 2004 with a child included.

** The law is uncertain on whether private fostering counts as work.

Fostering young people aged 16 and over

Fostering young people aged 16 and over is, in many ways, the same as fostering children under 16. If you cannot get benefits for them before the age of 16, you won't get benefits for them after the age of 16. The differences are given below.

Benefits for the carer

Child Benefit and Child Tax Credit

Once a child has reached the age of 16, these benefits can only be paid to the carer if the young person is still in full-time non-advanced education (meaning up to and including "A" level) or is 16 or 17 and has left education, registered for work with the Connexions Service and you apply within three months of education finishing.

Benefits for the young person

Most 16- and 17-year-olds cannot claim benefits. However, there are certain limited occasions where a young person may qualify for benefits in their own right.

Employment and Support Allowance

If the young person is unable to work due to sickness or disability, then they may qualify for Employment and Support Allowance. This benefit is not payable if the young person is in full-time education (meaning 21 hours a week). However, education that is intended only for people with a disability does not count towards the 21 hours.

Incapacity Benefit and/or Income Support (on the grounds of sickness)

Although these benefits have now been discontinued (to be replaced by Employment and Support Allowance), there are still some young people who are in receipt of these benefits.

Income Support

Some young people may qualify for Income Support if they are in full-time non-advanced education and they are estranged from their parents or anyone acting in place of the parents.

Jobseeker's Allowance

Some, but not many, young people qualify for Jobseeker's Allowance.

There are many 16–17-year-olds who will not qualify for these benefits, even if they are eligible. This is because it is still the responsibility of children's services to provide for maintenance and accommodation until they reach 18. If the young person was looked after for at least 13 weeks after their 14th birthday and before their 16th birthday, then the above benefits will not be payable (unless the young person is disabled or a single parent, in which case Income Support or Jobseeker's Allowance can continue).

Education Maintenance Allowance

This is an allowance of up to £30 a week to encourage young people to stay on at school or college. Young people who are looked after will get the full amount plus other bonuses depending on progression on the course.

BENEFITS SNAPSHOT:
FOSTERING YOUNG PEOPLE
AGED 16 AND OVER

	Can you claim extra for the child?	Do payments count as income?	Does fostering count as work?
Child Benefit	No	–	–
Income Support	No	No	No (?)
Housing Benefit	No	No	–
Council Tax Benefit	No	No	–
Jobseeker's Allowance	No	No	No
Council tax discounts	Yes (if child has disability)	–	–
Child Tax Credit	No	No	–
Working Tax Credit	–	No	Yes
Incapacity Benefit or Employment & Support Allowance	No	No	No (?)
Carer's Allowance	No	No	No
Pension Credit	No	No	–

Where a question mark appears (?) there is some doubt and it will also depend on whether the young person is looked after. Contact your social worker to have this checked out for you.

If you have your own children

Everything mentioned so far has focused on benefits for foster children. What follows now is the benefits available if you have your own children.

Child Benefit

The main rule for claiming Child Benefit is that you have a child or children living with you. There is no means-test involved, no national insurance contribution condition to be satisfied. Everyone with children can claim Child Benefit.

Child Tax Credit

Again, the main regulation for claiming Child Tax Credit is that you must have a child or children living with you. However, unlike Child Benefit, there is a means-test. If your yearly taxable income is less than £50,000, you will qualify for the basic amount of £10.50 a week. That amount will decrease the more your income goes up. Above £66,000, no Child Tax Credit will be payable.

Income Support or Jobseeker's Allowance

If you were in receipt of either of these benefits before April 2004 (with dependent child included in the claim), then you continue to get extra Income Support or Jobseeker's Allowance for your own children. You cannot claim extra benefits if you get Child Tax Credit. Single parents used to be able to claim

Income Support if their youngest child is under 16 but this has recently been reduced to 12. In future years, it will be reduced further.

Housing Benefit and Council Tax Benefit

Housing Benefit and Council Tax Benefit are determined by various factors including your income, rent and Council Tax and number of people in the household. You will be entitled to extra benefit for your own children.

Working Tax Credit

Although you cannot get extra Working Tax Credit because you have children (that is paid through Child Tax Credit), the presence of your children in the household is one of the grounds for claiming Working Tax Credit – you will, of course, have to be working for at least 16 hours a week.

Maintenance payments

If you are a lone parent and are receiving child support maintenance from the non-resident parent, the effect is as follows:

For Income Support and Jobseeker's Allowance (where the agreement began before 3 March 2003) the whole of the amount counts as income.

For Income Support and Jobseeker's Allowance (where the agreement began after 3 March 2003) the first £10 is ignored while the remainder counts.

For Housing Benefit and Council Tax Benefit (for under-60s) the first £15 is ignored whilst the remainder counts.

For Pension Credit, Housing Benefit and Council Tax Benefit (for over 60s) the whole amount is ignored.

For Child Tax Credit and Working Tax Credit the whole amount is ignored.

Education Maintenance Allowance

After the age of 16 your child may be able to claim an Educational Maintenance Allowance worth up to £30 a week, which is designed to encourage young people to stay on at school or college. It is dependent on your income. Only taxable income is taken into account so fostering allowance and s17 payments do not affect it.

CASE STUDY: **OWN CHILDREN**

Daphne is a single parent with two children aged 15 and 11 (as well as being a foster carer). She gets Child Benefit of £33.20 a week and £96.44 a week Child Tax Credit (for her two birth children, NOT the foster children). She will also get Income Support of £64.30. She needs to be aware that once the youngest child reaches 12, she will no longer be able to claim Income Support as a single parent but could claim as a foster carer.

BENEFITS SNAPSHOT: **IF YOU HAVE YOUR** **OWN CHILDREN**	Can you claim extra for the child?
Child Benefit	Yes
Income Support	No (?)
Housing Benefit	Yes
Council Tax Benefit	Yes
Jobseeker's Allowance	No (?)
Council tax discounts	Yes
Child Tax Credit	Yes
Working Tax Credit	–
Incapacity Benefit or Employment & Support Allowance	No
Carer's Allowance	No
Pension Credit	No

Where a question mark appears (?) there is some doubt. Contact your social worker to have this checked out for you.

If the child has a disability

10

If the child has a disability then there is extra help that you may be able to claim. This chapter applies to your own children and most forms of fostering – placements under s23, private and kinship care. However, it does not apply to respite and day care placements as the child does not live with you. You could still get Disability Living Allowance in parent and baby placements, although the limited nature of the placement may mean that another person is already claiming it.

Disability Living Allowance

See page 17 for the criteria for claiming Disability Living Allowance.

Although the benefit is payable *for* the child, it is payable *to* the parent/guardian. It is intended to meet the extra costs of having a disabled child in the household. Although the Department for Work & Pensions generally does not check on how the benefit is used, it's a good idea to keep a detailed account as the local authority may ask you to justify your expenditure.

Carer's Allowance

See page 16 for the criteria for claiming Carer's Allowance.

If the foster child gets the middle or high rate of the care component of Disability Living Allowance, you may be able to claim Carer's Allowance.

Council tax

This applies to all forms of fostering mentioned in this book apart from respite care, day care fostering and possibly parent and baby placements. It is only relevant if you are liable to pay council tax. If you have no council tax to pay (because, for example, you already get 100% Council Tax Benefit) or you are not liable (because, for example, you live with somebody else in their home) then this does not apply to you.

There are two situations (other than Council Tax Benefit) in which it may be possible to reduce your council tax liability: council tax disability reduction and status discount. They are not well known. Even though they are not benefits as such, they are mentioned here as another way of reducing your council tax liability.

To qualify for either of these schemes, your home must be the sole or main residence of the disabled person. This will be the case for most foster children.

Council tax disability reduction

Having a disabled person in the property may have an impact on your council tax. For the reduction to apply, the property must be the sole or main residence of a substantially and permanently disabled person (we will assume here that it is the foster child who has the disability; although it can be anybody living in the property). The use of the word "permanent" does not mean that the child will never get better; however, the reduction should not be granted for a short-term disability, no matter how severe.

The property must have one of the following features:

- a room (but not bathroom, kitchen or lavatory) used predominantly by the disabled person; or

- an additional bathroom or kitchen necessary for meeting the needs of the disabled person; or

- sufficient floor space to permit the use of a wheelchair.

The feature must be of major importance to the disabled person's well-being. When deciding whether to apply for the disability reduction, the question is:

Would the disabled person find it impossible or extremely difficult to continue living here or would their health suffer without the feature?

If your application is successful, a disability reduction will drop your council tax liability by one band. Residents in Band A properties will get a reduction of an amount equivalent to five-ninths of the amount payable in Band D properties.

Another major advantage of the disability reduction scheme is that the local authority can backdate the reduction (unlike most benefits). In theory, if you are eligible for the reduction from April 1993 (when council tax was introduced), then it can be awarded from 1993/4.

You should request the backdating to the latest of the following three dates: the date the child came to live with you; the date the adaptations mentioned above were done to the property; or 1 April 1993. However, the local council may object to this interpretation and attempt to limit the amount of backdating. You may have a challenge on your hands.

Another problem with the disability reduction is that your property must be the sole or main residence of the disabled person. If it is a parent and baby placement and the parent and baby have a home elsewhere, for example, it may be difficult to prove that your home is their main residence.

A suggested sample letter is provided in Appendix 3.

Council tax carer's discount

Another way of reducing your council tax liability, the carer's discount, is also linked to having a disabled person living in your property.

This applies to all forms of fostering mentioned in this book apart from respite care and day care fostering. It is only relevant if you are liable to pay council tax. If you have no council tax to pay (because, for example, you already get 100% Council Tax Benefit) or you are not liable (because, for example, you live with somebody else in their home), then this does not apply to you.

Council tax liability is based on the assumption that there are two adults living in the property. If there is only one adult treated as living in the property, you are entitled to a 25% discount. If there are no adults treated as living in the property you are entitled to a 50% discount. There is a long list of people to be disregarded for living in the property but the one that is of relevance to us is the carer's discount.

You can be treated as *not* living in the property if you meet the following criteria:

- you are resident in the same property as the person being cared for;

- you are providing care for at least 35 hours a week;

- you are not the partner or parent (if the disabled person is under 18) of the person needing care;

- you are caring for somebody entitled to the high rate of the care component of Disability Living Allowance.

Another major advantage of the discount scheme is that the local council can backdate the discount (unlike most benefits). In theory, if you are eligible for the discount from April 1993 (when council tax was introduced), then it can be awarded from 1993/4.

You should request the backdating to the latest of the following three dates: the date the child came to live with you; the date the child was awarded the high rate of the care component of Disability Living Allowance; or 1 April 1993. However, as with the council tax reduction, the local council may attempt to limit the amount of backdating. If you are refused what you believe you are entitled to, seek advice – for instance, from a Citizens Advice Bureau or legal centre.

Disabled facilities grant

What is it?
To help meet the cost of adapting a property for the needs of a disabled person.

Who is it for?

The owner occupier or tenant applies but the grant is to help the disabled person live in the property. It is not means-tested if the application is made by the guardian of a disabled child (that includes you as a foster carer).

How to claim

Contact your local council.

CASE STUDY: **FOSTERING A DISABLED CHILD**

Ryan is a seven-year-old boy with quite severe and challenging behavioural problems. He lives with his foster carers. Because he requires continual supervision by day and night, he is awarded the high rate of the care component of Disability Living Allowance. One of the foster carers can claim Carer's Allowance. As they both provide 35 hours a week care, they can both be classed as carers and get a 50% discount on their council tax.

BENEFITS SNAPSHOT:
IF THE CHILD HAS
A DISABILITY

	Can you claim extra for the child?	Do payments count as income?	Does fostering count as work?
Child Benefit	No	–	–
Income Support	No	No	No (?)
Housing Benefit	No	No	–
Council Tax Benefit	No	No	–
Jobseeker's Allowance	No	No	No
Council tax discounts	Yes	–	–
Child Tax Credit	No	No	–
Working Tax Credit	–	No	Yes
Incapacity Benefit or Employment & Support Allowance	No	No	No (?)
Carer's Allowance	Yes	No	No
Pension Credit	No	No	–

Where a question mark appears (?) there is some doubt and it also depends on the status of the child. Contact your social worker to have this checked out for you.

Appendix 1:
Other reading material

Welfare Benefits and Tax Credits Handbook 2009–10, from Child Poverty Action Group, is the most comprehensive book on benefits and tax credits. It costs £37 (or £8.50 for individual benefit claimants).

Council Tax Handbook 2009, also from Child Poverty Action Group, gives all the rules on liability for council tax and discounts and reductions. It costs £17.00.

To order either of these, go to *www.cpag.org.uk* to download an order form or phone 020 7837 7979.

Disability Rights Handbook (April 2008–April 2009) from Disability Alliance covers benefits, tax and social services. The CD-ROM version costs £20 or £15.50 if you are on benefits. The print version costs £17 or £14 if you are on benefits.

See *www.disabilityalliance.org* or phone 020 7247 8776.

Appendix 2

Use this sample letter to apply for council tax disability reduction.

To: local council

Date:

Dear Sir/Madam

Re: (your name and address)

Council tax reference number:

I wish to ask for a disability reduction for the above named property.

Name of child, who is resident in the above address, has a permanent and substantial disability. The property has the following feature:

- A room used predominantly by *name of child**
- An additional bathroom or kitchen needed by *name of child**
- Sufficient floor space to permit the use of a wheelchair*

Name of child would find it extremely difficult to continue living there/ impossible to continue living there/health would suffer* without the feature. It is of essential or major importance to his/her* well-being.

I wish to request this application to be backdated to *date*.

Yours sincerely

Words in *italics* – substitute your own details

*delete the word/phrase that does not apply

Appendix 3

Use this sample letter to apply for council tax status discount.

To: local council

Date:

Dear Sir/Madam

Re: (your name and address)

Council tax reference number:

I wish to ask for a carer's discount for the above named property.

Name(s) of carer(s) provides care and support to *name of child* for at least 35 hours a week. *Name(s) of carer(s)* is/are* resident in the same dwelling as *name of child*. *Name(s) of carer(s)* is/are* not the parent of *name of child*, who gets the high rate of the care component of Disability Living Allowance.

I wish to ask for the carer's discount to be backdated to *date*.

Yours sincerely

Words in *italics* – substitute your own details

*delete the word/phrase that does not apply

Index

Compiled by Elisabeth Pickard